PEOPLE & PLACES

Japan

D1289433

Written by

Steve Parker

Consultant Kyoko Read

Illustrated by

Ann Savage

SILVER BURDETT PRESS
MORRISTOWN, NEW JERSEY

Editor Steve Parker
Editor, U.S. Edition Joanne Fink
Designer Patrick Nugent
Photo-researcher Hugh Olliff
Studio services Kenneth Ward

A TEMPLAR BOOK

Devised and produced by Templar Publishing Ltd
107 High Street, Dorking, Surrey, England, RH4 1QA

Adapted and first published in the United States
in 1988 by Silver Burdett Press, Morristown, N.J.

Color separations by Positive Colour Ltd, Maldon, Essex, England
Printed by L.E.G.O., Vicenza, Italy

Library of Congress Cataloging-in-Publication Data

Parker, Steve.
  Japan / written by Steve Parker : consultant, Kyoko Read :
illustrated by Ann Savage.
      p.   cm. — (People and places)
  "A Templar book" — T.p. verso
  Includes index
  Summary: Text and pictures introduce the geography, history,
people, and culture of Japan.
  ISBN 0-382-09504-9
1. Japan—Juvenile literature.   [1. Japan.]   I. Savage, Ann.
ill.   II. Title.   III. Series: People and places (Morristown,
N.J.)
DS806.P38 1988
952—dc19   87-28521
                                                   CIP
                                                    AC

Contents

WHERE IN THE WORLD?

Spin a globe and find Japan. It is in the Far East, off the eastern coasts of Korea and the Soviet Union. It is not one single land mass but a string of islands, four large and many small. These islands stretch for 2,400 miles down the northwestern side of the Pacific Ocean.

Japan may not look very large on a map. But in land area it is half as big again as the United Kingdom. In fact it is larger than all European countries except Spain, France and Sweden. Even so, Japan is only one-twentieth as big as Australia and one-twenty-fifth the size of the United States.

Japan's history goes back many centuries. The Japanese developed one of the world's earliest civilizations. Some 9,000 years ago, they were making earthenware pots and decorative plaques and figures. At that time they lived mainly by hunting and fishing. About 2,300 years ago the Japanese were growing rice, using iron tools, and weaving cloth. Over the past 1,200 years Japanese books recorded many exciting events, as emperors and *shoguns* (warlords) fought to control the country.

A medieval warrior in traditional costume.

Symbols of Japan

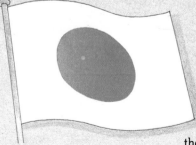

The Japanese flag is a red circle on a white background. It represents the rising sun, to remind the Japanese people that every day brings new opportunities. The word "Japan" comes from *Jipanqu*, the name given to the country by the explorer Marco Polo.

Mount Fuji, 12,389 feet high, is Japan's tallest mountain. It is a dormant ("sleeping") volcano, 68 miles southwest of Tokyo.

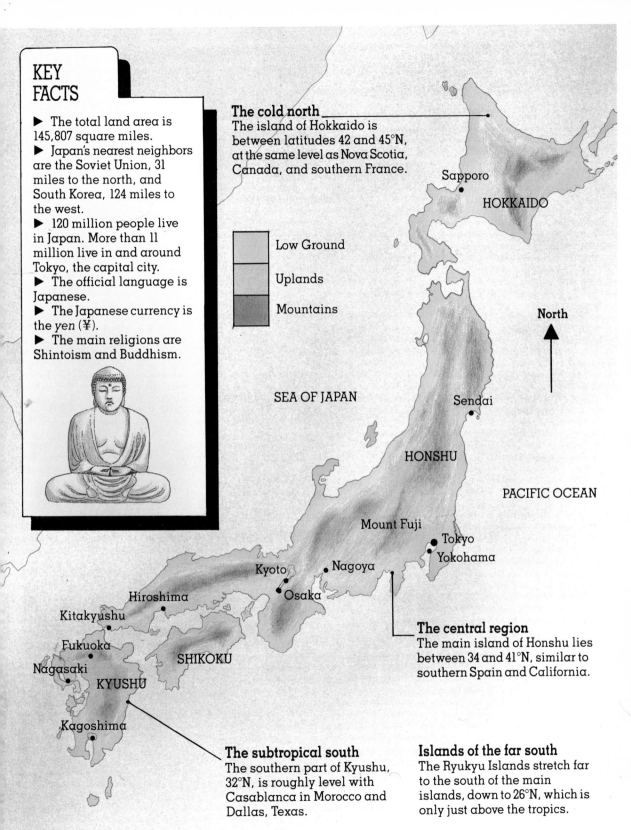

KEY FACTS

▶ The total land area is 145,807 square miles.

▶ Japan's nearest neighbors are the Soviet Union, 31 miles to the north, and South Korea, 124 miles to the west.

▶ 120 million people live in Japan. More than 11 million live in and around Tokyo, the capital city.

▶ The official language is Japanese.

▶ The Japanese currency is the yen (¥).

▶ The main religions are Shintoism and Buddhism.

The cold north
The island of Hokkaido is between latitudes 42 and 45°N, at the same level as Nova Scotia, Canada, and southern France.

Low Ground

Uplands

Mountains

SEA OF JAPAN

North

Sapporo

HOKKAIDO

Sendai

HONSHU

PACIFIC OCEAN

Mount Fuji

Tokyo

Yokohama

Nagoya

Kyoto

Osaka

Hiroshima

Kitakyushu

Fukuoka

Nagasaki

SHIKOKU

KYUSHU

Kagoshima

The central region
The main island of Honshu lies between 34 and 41°N, similar to southern Spain and California.

The subtropical south
The southern part of Kyushu, 32°N, is roughly level with Casablanca in Morocco and Dallas, Texas.

Islands of the far south
The Ryukyu Islands stretch far to the south of the main islands, down to 26°N, which is only just above the tropics.

THE LANGUAGE OF JAPAN

T he Japanese language is regarded by many experts as one of the most complicated languages in the world. It does not have a simple alphabet of around 20 or 30 letters, as in English or French. Instead, there are hundreds of characters, developed by the Japanese from the old Chinese written language. Some of these characters were "pictograms," small pictures representing objects such as a tree or house. Other characters represented ideas, such as good or bad.

Tree

The Japanese have added two sets of "phonetic signs" to their characters. These signs show how the characters should be pronounced. In each set there are 46 phonetic signs. Students must learn some 2,000 characters, and the two sets of phonetic signs, in order to read, write, and speak Japanese well.

Today most Japanese schoolchildren learn to read and write in English as well as in Japanese. This is important for their country's role in the modern world, especially as a trading nation. In many large Japanese cities the signposts, notices, and advertisements are in both Japanese and English.

Cedar tree

Pictures for words
In Japanese, there is one basic character which means the same as the English word "tree." The names for certain types of tree are shown by adding other symbols to this character. In a similar way, the English language adds extra words, for example "pine tree."

Pine tree

The art of writing

Many Japanese children learn to draw the characters of their language with great style and beauty. It is a natural part of their artistic tradition. The skillful use of the brush or pen in this way is called *shuji* or *shodo*. It is known as calligraphy in English.

Signs of the times

Neon signs shine late at night in the busy Shinjukudori shopping area of Tokyo. Some English words can be seen among the many advertisements and store names in Japanese.

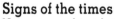

9

WHAT'S THE WEATHER LIKE?

Japan's climate is roughly the same as a north–south strip of America's Midwest or Central Europe. It's cool in the north, mild in the middle, and warm in the south. There are four seasons, but the farther south you go, the more these merge into each other.

Besides this north–south difference, there is also an east–west difference. In winter, cold winds blow southeastward from central Asia, bringing much rain and snow to Japan's west coast. The high mountains of central Japan protect the eastern, Pacific coast from the worst of this weather, and winters there are dry, cold, and clear.

Summer weather is the opposite. Warm winds blow across the country northwestward from the Pacific Ocean, bringing rain to the eastern side. On the Pacific coast, people expect three or four weeks of rain during June and early July.

Sports in snow and sun
In winter, resorts in the mountains above Tokyo, and on northern Honshu and Hokkaido, swish with the sounds of skis and ice skates. At the same time in Naha, Okinawa (one of the most southern islands), people are sunbathing and swimming.

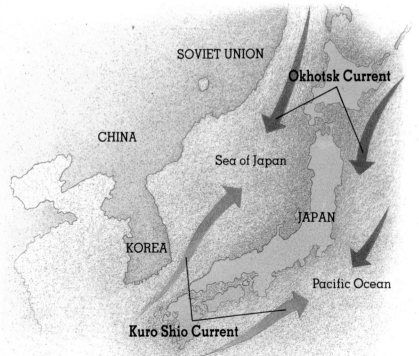

Seas blowing hot and cold
Two ocean currents have effects on the Japanese climate. The Okhotsk Current brings down icy waters from the north, adding to Hokkaido's cold winters. The Kuro Shio Current brings up warm waters from the tropics, making winters in the south just a bit warmer.

The heralds of spring

In March and April, after the long cold winter, peach and cherry trees blossom all over Japan. This is a time of rejoicing and flower festivals.

Cool and refreshing

During September and October the hot, humid days come to an end. In the hill country, the dark greens of the pine trees show up against the brilliant reds, oranges, and golds of the broadleaved trees.

KEY FACTS

Lows and highs

▶ In Sapporo, on Hokkaido in the far north, the average January temperature is 20°F. In July it is 68°F.

▶ In Tokyo, it is milder all year round. The average temperatures are 39°F for January and 77°F for July.

▶ Kagoshima, down south, is even warmer. It rises from almost 45°F in January to 80°F in July.

FROM COUNTRY TO CITY

T hree-quarters of Japan is covered with steep mountains, mostly cloaked in forests, where few people dwell. Three-quarters of the people live on the narrow coastal plains, in the ports, cities, and towns. Seven of the biggest cities are on the main island, Honshu. Tokyo is the biggest – the center of Japanese business and culture. With over 11 million people packed into 784 square miles, Tokyo is probably the most crowded city on earth – as well as the second largest, after Mexico City.

As more and more people move from country to city, the cities spread. Tokyo is slowly becoming joined to Yokohama, the second biggest Japanese city with a population of nearly three million. In the whole of the Tokyo/Yokohama built-up area there are over 26 million people!

Compare this with the northern island of Hokkaido. The largest city here is Sapporo, with one and a half million people. Nearly three-quarters of the island is given over to prairie crops, or is left as natural moors, mountains, and forests, and is almost empty of people. It's where many Japanese themselves go for vacations.

Faces in the crowd
In Tokyo the streets are filled with factory workers, office staff, shoppers, and visitors.

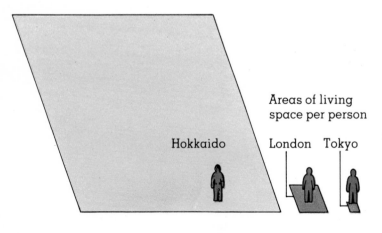

Areas of living space per person

Hokkaido   London   Tokyo

Packed with people
Tokyo is one of the world's most crowded places. On the average, each resident has 1,000 square feet of living space. This is only a third as much as in other capital cities, such as London. Yet on Japan's northern island, Hokkaido, one person has an average of 140,000 square feet.

A day in the city

Trains to Sendai's railroad station bring thousands of workers to their jobs in the city's high-rise office buildings and factories.

The building of Japan

The islands of Japan are the peaks of underwater mountains, rising from a very deep sea bed. They are at the place where two of the great slabs, or plates, that make up the Earth's surface, have rubbed against each other. As the plates pressed together over millions of years, their edges buckled to make the mountains. We see evidence of this in Japan's 50 or so active volcanoes and the 1,500 small earthquakes each year.

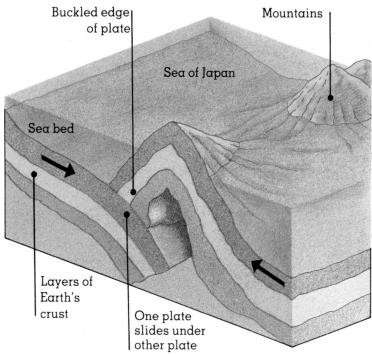

Buckled edge of plate

Mountains

Sea of Japan

Sea bed

Layers of Earth's crust

One plate slides under other plate

TRAVELING IN JAPAN

L ike any modern country, Japan is criss-crossed by roads and railways. Since Japan is an island nation, there are ferry boats chugging to and fro along the coasts. As the pace of life speeds up, more and more people use planes to get from city to city. With the importance of Japan's overseas trade, the international airports at Tokyo and Osaka are always busy. Every day the buses and subways carry millions of people from the suburbs where they live to their jobs in the big cities. In Japan, people are always going somewhere.

Before 1971, most passengers used the trains. After that time, the roads took over. Freight traffic has followed the same pattern, with more freight now traveling by road than by rail. However, Japanese railways are fighting back with new lines, trains, and services. In crowded Japan, many people believe it's best to use the railway lines already there, rather than build new roads on land that would be better kept for farming and houses.

Sardine time
There are subways in eight large Japanese cities. In Tokyo alone there are 10 lines with over 125 miles of track. During the rush hour, millions of people cram into the trains. For the visitor, it can be a frightening experience.

The "bullet train"
Japan's inter-city trains are among the fastest, cleanest, and most comfortable in the world. Also, they are hardly ever late! The *Shinkansen* super-express trains can travel at 155 miles per hour.

The right road?
New roads are being built all over Japan. Often they have to run on valuable coastal land, or through city centers. Here expressways and overpasses run alongside a river on the outskirts of Sendai.

Sapporo •

Seikan Tunnel

•Sendai
Niigata •

Oshimizu Tunnel

•Tokyo
Kyoto Nagoya •Yokohama
Hiroshima • •Osaka
Kitakyushu•
Fukuoka•

Kagoshima•

—— Major roads
—— Main railway services
—— Inter-city trains
—— Air routes
—— Ferry services

Taking to the air
Japanese Air Lines, whose symbol you can see above, is the third-biggest international airline. Its planes fly all over the world as well as to major Japanese cities. All-Nippon Airways has routes to many Japanese cities. Toa Domestic Airlines flies shorter local trips.

Island-hopping
Ferries of all shapes and sizes sail between the four main islands and the many smaller ones. They carry people, cars, trucks, and trains. The most modern services use hovercrafts and hydrofoils, though a few sailing boats still exist.

KEY FACTS
Japan has the world's longest railroad tunnel under mountains, and the longest railroad tunnel under the sea.
▶ The Oshimizu Tunnel carries the Tokyo-Niigata line under the Tanigawa mountains. It is 13.7 miles long.
▶ The Seikan Tunnel runs under the sea between northern Honshu and Hokkaido. It is 33.4 miles long.

15

THE LAND SHAPES THE NATION

Hardly anywhere in Japan is far from the mountains or the sea. This fact, more than any other, has shaped the way people live and work. The mountains of inland Japan mean that little of the land can be farmed for food (though some of the upland forests are cut for timber). Most farming is done on the narrow coastal plains, which are also crowded with people. The Japanese do not have enough land to grow their food.

The sea helps out, to an extent. Japan is the greatest fishing nation in the world (see page 22). But this alone is not enough. Japan must buy basic foods from other countries. It has few natural resources either, some coal and precious metals, and hardly any oil.

Faced with the problem of how to feed their growing population and buy the raw materials they need, the Japanese have turned to industry. They have become one of the greatest industrial and manufacturing nations in the world.

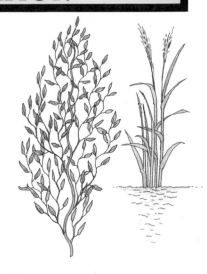

Raising rice
Rice is one of Japan's favorite foods. Rice seedlings are raised in seedbeds, then planted out in the rains of June and July. The flooded fields where the rice is grown are called *tanbo*. Every spare piece of land is levelled, planted with rice, and kept flooded until the autumn harvest.

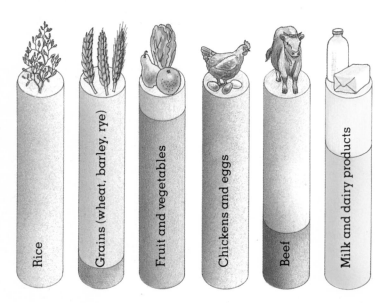

Rice

Grains (wheat, barley, rye)

Fruit and vegetables

Chickens and eggs

Beef

Milk and dairy products

Japan's food bill
Japan imports most of its basic foods from other countries, especially America, Canada, and Australia. The chart on the left shows how much of each food Japan grows (darker portion) and how much it buys from abroad (lighter portion). More and more Japanese are turning to Western-type foods, such as bread made from wheat, and are eating less traditional food such as rice.

Smooth as silk

In the past, millions of silkworms spun the world-famous Japanese silk used in beautiful *kimonos* and other fine clothes. The "worms" are actually moth caterpillars and they eat mulberry leaves. Today there are fewer silkworm farms, because silk imported from abroad costs less than Japanese silk. Also, more clothes are now made from artificial fibers.

Silkworm (caterpillar)

Silk cocoon

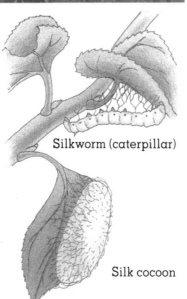

17

THE POWER FOR INDUSTRY

Imported oil and coal fuel the furnaces and factories of Japan's great industrial machine. They provide over three-quarters of the nation's energy. Oil comes mostly from the Middle East, while coal comes from Australia, the United States, and Canada.

The Japanese wish to cut their oil and coal bills. They do not want to rely so heavily on these sources of energy, with supplies under the control of other countries. Instead, they want to make their own energy. Over 30 nuclear power stations have been built, and the aim is for nuclear power to supply one-seventh of Japan's energy needs by the year 2000. By then, oil should provide less than one-half of the country's energy. There is also hydroelectric power from the fast, shallow rivers.

Research into solar (sun) power, and wind and wave power is already underway. Many Japanese people are anxious to see these energy sources become more important, since they are generally cleaner and safer than oil or nuclear power.

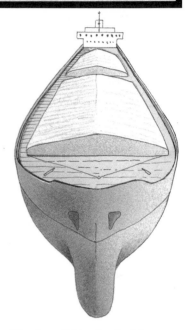

Black gold in the hold
Japanese boatyards build more than half of the world's ships (in terms of weight). The ships include the largest ones of all, the oil-carrying supertankers weighing half a million tons.

Oiling the wheels
Oil depots and refineries line many deep-water ports. The oil is used for power, and is also refined to make plastics and other raw materials for industry.

Industry's ins and outs

Japan relies heavily on oil to provide the electricity and heating needed by its factories, offices, and homes. Over half of all energy is used by industry.

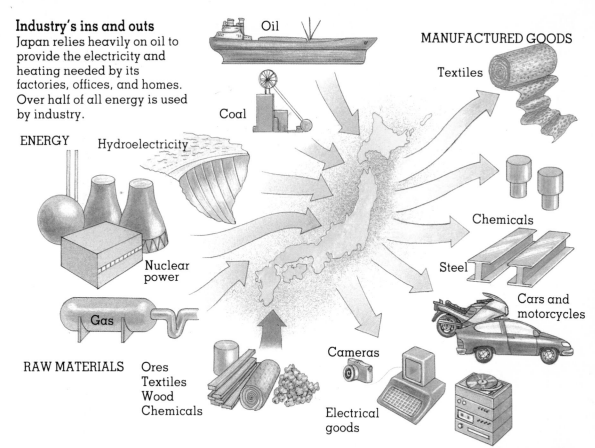

Oil

Coal

MANUFACTURED GOODS

Textiles

ENERGY

Hydroelectricity

Nuclear power

Gas

Chemicals

Steel

Cars and motorcycles

Cameras

Electrical goods

RAW MATERIALS   Ores
Textiles
Wood
Chemicals

Making metals

The vast Mizushima Steelworks is part of the Kawasaki Iron and Steel Company. (Japanese companies are often named after the cities where they were originally based.) Iron and other ores are brought in by bulk on cargo ships. The ores are made into high-grade steel and other special metals, for use by Japanese factories and also to be sold abroad.

"MADE IN JAPAN"

L ook around your home or school and you will almost certainly find the "Made in Japan" label on something. From ships and cars to cameras and microprocessors for computers, Japan makes them all.

Besides making finished goods, the Japanese also provide materials in bulk to the industries of other countries. Japanese chemicals, steel and special metals go to factories all over the world. Often the machinery in these factories, and even the workers' clothes, were made in Japan. Japan has an enormous share of world trade for a small country, producing about one-fifteenth of all world exports.

Other countries make the same types of goods as Japan, but the Japanese versions are often better and cheaper. Some countries complain that Japan puts their own workers out of jobs. They may refuse to buy goods from Japan, or add taxes to Japanese goods to make them more expensive. Discussions and trade agreements between governments are sometimes needed to solve the problems.

Small companies
More than half of the Japanese goods sold abroad are made by small and medium-sized companies, with less than 300 employees.

Japan's trading partners
The country that buys most goods from Japan is America. Britain, West Germany, France, and other countries in Western Europe together take over one-tenth of the Japanese exports. China, South Korea, and Taiwan also import many Japanese goods.

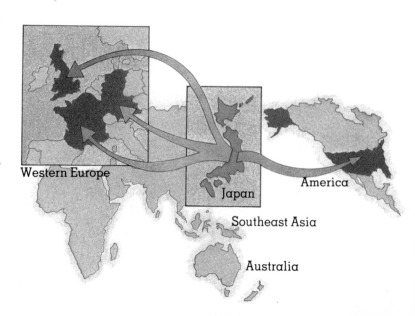

Western Europe

Japan

America

Southeast Asia

Australia

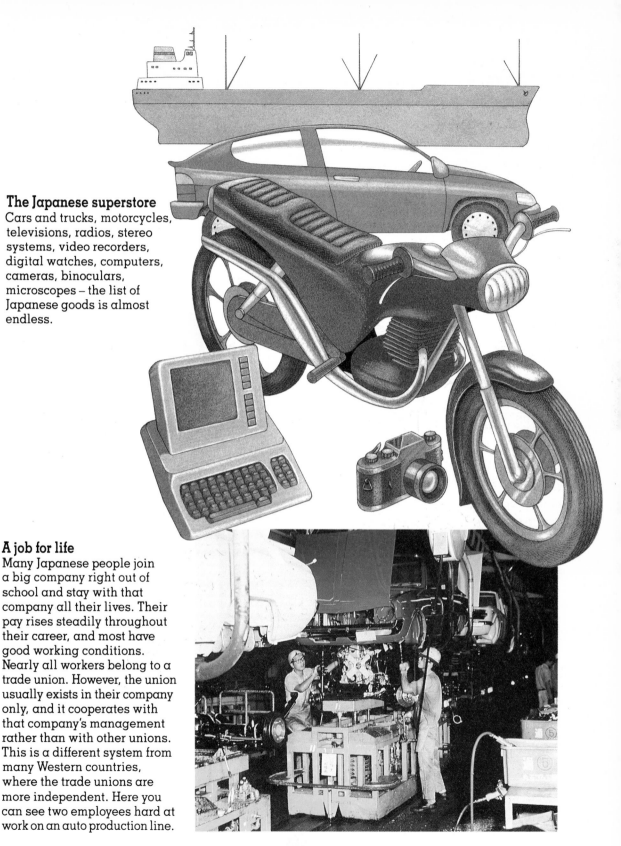

The Japanese superstore

Cars and trucks, motorcycles, televisions, radios, stereo systems, video recorders, digital watches, computers, cameras, binoculars, microscopes – the list of Japanese goods is almost endless.

A job for life

Many Japanese people join a big company right out of school and stay with that company all their lives. Their pay rises steadily throughout their career, and most have good working conditions. Nearly all workers belong to a trade union. However, the union usually exists in their company only, and it cooperates with that company's management rather than with other unions. This is a different system from many Western countries, where the trade unions are more independent. Here you can see two employees hard at work on an auto production line.

HARVESTING THE SEAS

The Japanese have always caught and eaten fish. In the small towns and villages dotted along the coast, families lived by fishing from small boats. In some areas this old way of life still goes on. But much of Japan's fish is now caught by fleets of huge trawlers that trail their nets through the world's oceans. In their search for shoals of herring, sardine, anchovy, cod, haddock, mackerel, and tuna, the boats go as far as the Arctic and Antarctic. They unload their fish at sea onto giant factory ships, which clean and process them, and freeze or can them on the spot.

In recent years, many countries have announced a 200-mile limit around their shores. Fishing by other countries is not allowed inside the limit. Since most fish are caught near land, this has caused great problems for the Japanese fishing fleets. Another problem is that boats have become too good at finding and catching fish so the number of fish is declining. Pollution is also affecting coastal waters. Japan now imports more fish than ever before.

Saving the whale
Some types of whales are in danger of extinction because of hunting. In 1987 Japan joined with nearly all other countries in the world and stopped large-scale whaling. However, the Japanese had one of the largest whaling fleets in the world. Now, many people who worked on the ships and in the whale-processing factories are out of work.

The tuna boats
Fishermen and their boats rest between trips, moored at Yaidu Port. Such boats may travel thousands of miles in their search for tuna (tunny), one of the world's most important food fish.

The world's fisheries

The oceans, especially around Japan, were once rich in herring, cod, sardine, tuna, and mackerel. Now the catches are smaller because of over-fishing. Here are some of the main fishing grounds around Japan.

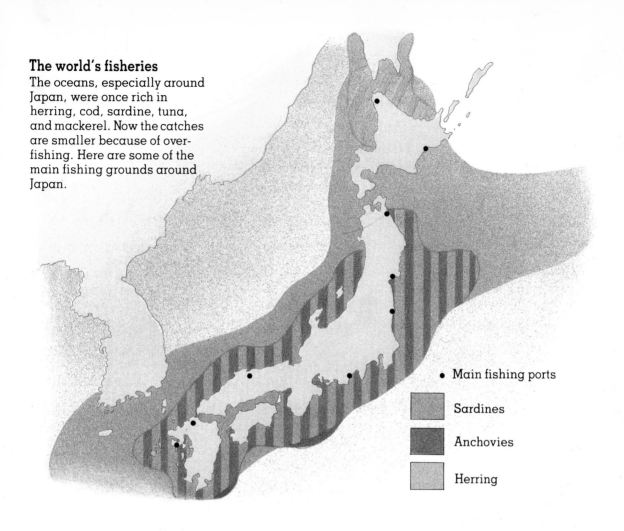

● Main fishing ports

Sardines

Anchovies

Herring

Fresh from the sea

Traditional Japanese dishes such as *sashimi* and *sushi* feature the delicate flavors of raw fish. Fish is a major source of protein in the Japanese diet.

A WILDERNESS FOR WILDLIFE

Japan's trees, flowers, animals, and birds have suffered in the past. Houses, factories, and roads have spread across the coastal plains and into the mountains, eating into the natural areas where wildlife once lived. The air around the cities, especially Tokyo, was heavy with smog from the fumes of cars, trucks, factory chimneys, and power stations. Coastal waters were polluted by the industrial wastes pouring from shore pipelines. However, in recent years there have been many restrictions on pollution, so that the air and water are becoming cleaner.

Tokyo Bay shows how the situation is improving. This bay used to be one of the most polluted bodies of water around Japan. The dumping of wastes is now controlled and the waters have become clear again. Seaweed and fish that had died out are slowly returning. Local boatmen are once again making a living from fishing in the bay, and collecting shellfish and seaweed to eat. Hopefully the clean-up campaigns will continue and Japan's wildlife will make a comeback.

The snow monkeys

Japanese macaque monkeys live in bands a hundred or more strong. They inhabit forests and the seashore, and their thick fur protects them from the winter cold. Scientists have studied them for many years, to learn about group behavior. One monkey started to clean her food by washing it in the sea – and the others soon began to copy this trick. They avoid the cold by sitting in the natural hot-water springs that bubble up through the rocks.

Record-breaking crab

The Japanese spider-crab is the world's largest crab. It is trawled up from the deep waters off the southeast coast. It can measure over 11 feet from claw to claw! Normally it is supported by the water. When taken out, its muscles are so weak that it can hardly move.

Using nature's fisherman

Cormorants are common seabirds in many parts of the world, including Japan. In the old days they were trained to dive for fish while on a line, and bring the fish to the boat. A ring around the bird's neck prevented it from swallowing the fish. There are still trained cormorants today, such as at Gifa near Nagoya, but they are mainly for tourists.

Dancing in the snow

Japanese cranes are among the rarest birds in the world. About 75 years ago they had almost died out. However, the people of Hokkaido fed them through the winters, and there are now more than 400 cranes on this island. In early spring the male and female birds leap up and down and flap their wings in a mating dance.

LANDS OF THE EMPEROR

Japan has an exciting and complicated history. For many centuries emperors had absolute power over the people. As in many other countries, they often used force to bring their people under control. However, the mountains and the sea passages between the islands meant that Japan was not always one nation. For long periods the emperors lost control of remote or mountainous areas. Warlords, chieftains, and barons fought each other in the countryside, and treated the ordinary people badly.

During the middle ages Japan had a "twin government" of emperor and *shogun*. The shogun was the "generalissimo" or military leader. The emperor was supposed to appoint the shogun and have overall power. More often, though, the emperor ruled over his court while the shogun ruled over the rest of Japan.

Capitals through the ages

The Japanese have had many capital cities during their long and colorful history. It seems unthinkable that today's capital would ever move from Tokyo – but the ancient people thought their capitals would never move, either!

Nara (710–784)
Nara was the first permanent capital, created in the early days of Japanese Buddhism. Several emperors had their courts here, and beautiful temples were built in Buddha's honor. The first written records, the *Kojikui* ("Records of Ancient Matters"), date from 712.

Kyoto (794–1192)
A new city was built at Heian-kyo ("Capital of peace and tranquillity"), later to become part of Kyoto. Like Nara, the city had a right-angled street plan, copying the Chinese style of Chang'an. Emperors ruled over this time of great prosperity, the Heian Period.

Kyoto (Muromachi) ●
Nara ●

Edo (1603–1867)

The *shogun* Tokugawa Ieyasu gained control of all Japan and set up his military government at Edo, which today is called Tokyo. Peace returned to much of Japan. But the rulers were worried about Christianity taking over from traditional religions. From 1639 the shogun cut off Japan from the rest of the world. Japan stayed isolated during the Tokugawa Period, for over 200 years.

Tokyo (1868–today)

In the mid-19th century Japan was pushed out of its isolation because of increased trading with the West, but the government weakened. From 1867 an emperor once again ruled Japan. Mutsuhito Meiji held the title for 43 years. He moved his court from Kyoto to Edo, which was renamed Tokyo ("Eastern capital").

Warriors by trade

During the Tokugawa Period the people were divided into four classes: *samurai*, peasants, craftsmen, and merchants. Samurai (meaning "servants") were the only ones allowed to carry two swords, traditionally a long one and a short one. In return for land to farm or a well-paid job, the samurai had to fight when and where they were needed. The title went from father to son. Over the years the samurai built a strict code of loyalty, bravery, and honor. Rather than be disgraced and break his code, a true samurai would kill himself by slitting his belly with a knife.

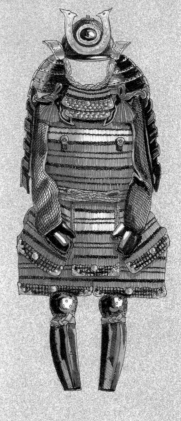

Kamakura (1192–1333)

Wars between various clans brought the Heian Period to a bloody end. Yoritomo of the Minamoto (Genji) Clan took power and with the "permission" of the emperor (who was only 13 years old) he set up government at Kamakura. Military leaders ruled Japan for almost 700 years.

Tokyo
■ (Edo)
● Kamakura

Muromachi (1336–1603)

The Ashikaga Clan moved the capital to Muromachi, Kyoto. This was the time of the *shoguns*, who built great villas, castles, and temples. After a time the central rulers lost much of their power and the country went back to the feudal system, where local *daimyo* (warlords) had complete power in the region.

The U.S. enters World War II

On December 7, 1941, Japanese planes bombed American warships moored at their Hawaiian base of Pearl Harbor. It was a savage and sudden attack, and war was declared immediately.

The Japanese fight on...

Japanese soldiers were feared the world over for their fighting spirit. They admired the samurai code of *bushido*, battling with amazing ferocity and always to the death. In this photograph, taken during the war, they have captured an enemy gun position.

I n July, 1853, a fleet of four ships sailed into the Japanese port of Uraga. The commander was Commodore Matthew Perry of the U.S. Navy. His aim was to bring Japan out of her isolation and start trading agreements. He got no immediate answer from the shogun. But after several more visits and shows of force by American, British, and Russian fleets, Japan began to open up to foreign trade.

From that time until World War II ended in 1945, Japan was involved in several conflicts. In 1904 it fought Russia (and won). In World War I it joined the Allies (Britain, France and Russia) against Germany, and won. In the following years there were skirmishes with the Chinese about Manchuria, on the mainland. But gradually the Japanese government lost power to the army and navy. In 1937 the fight with China flared again, and Japan sided with Germany and Italy. The long history of Japanese pride and the *samurai* spirit were encouraged by the military leaders. The nation was told that Japan was unbeatable.

As World War II raged in Europe, Japan claimed to own territories in China and the Pacific. These claims were disputed by Britain, America, and Russia. Quickly the disputes became more serious. Suddenly, in 1941, Japan entered the war.

Japan during World War II

The Japanese Empire reached its greatest size in 1942, during World War II. For a few brief months Japan controlled much of Southeast Asia and the Pacific. The downfall of the Empire came when the U.S. Navy defeated the Japanese Navy at the Battle of Midway.

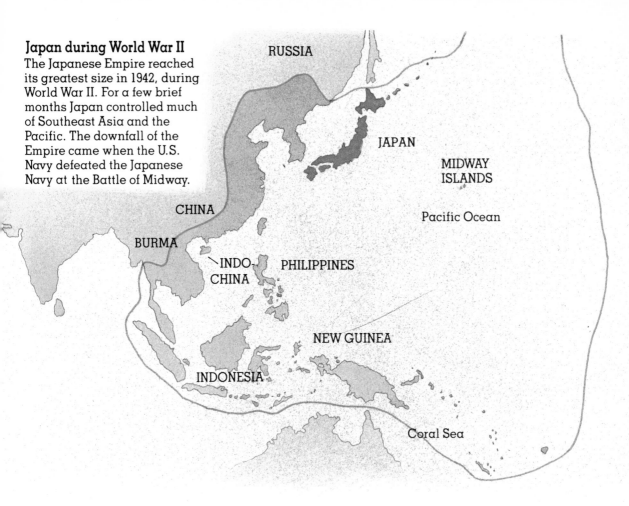

RUSSIA

JAPAN

MIDWAY ISLANDS

Pacific Ocean

CHINA

BURMA

INDO-CHINA

PHILIPPINES

NEW GUINEA

INDONESIA

Coral Sea

The bomb drops

Slowly the Allies began to push Japan back. But the end came through scientists rather than soldiers. In August 1945, two atomic bombs were dropped on Hiroshima and Nagasaki. The cities became deserts of destruction, as you can see here, and thousands died. The war was over.

GOVERNING JAPAN TODAY

J apan has recovered from the destruction of World War II. It now has a government elected by the people. The country is run in much the same way as the United States, Australia, Britain and many other countries.

The Japanese people vote to elect who represents them in the two houses of the Diet (the national parliament). They also elect their representatives on the Prefectures (regional councils) and on city, town, and village councils. Every citizen aged 20 years or over can vote in all these elections.

Japan's constitution, which is the framework of laws and regulations by which the country runs, came into being on May 3, 1947. At that time, although the emperor kept his title, he had no real power. In fact, the emperor now acts on behalf of the people in such matters as opening a new session of the Diet.

His Imperial Majesty
Emperor Hirohito was born in 1901 and took the throne in 1926. His official home is the Imperial Palace in Tokyo.

The seat of government
Japan's elected representatives meet in the National Diet, the government building in Tokyo.

KEY FACTS

There are six main political parties in the Diet:
► The Liberal Democratic Party. Its policies are similar to Britain's Conservatives and America's Republicans. It has governed since 1955 without a break
► The Japanese Socialists, the chief opposition party
► The Komeito (Clean Government Party)
► The Japanese Communists
► The New Liberal Club
► The Democratic Socialists

NATIONAL GOVERNMENT
Prime Minister
Leads the majority party in the Diet

Cabinet
19 Ministers appointed by the Prime Minister
Makes major decisions

IMPERIAL FAMILY
Emperor
Symbolic head of state
No political power

12 Ministries
Justice
Domestic Affairs
Foreign Affairs
Finance
Education
Health and Welfare
Agriculture, Forestry, and Fisheries
International Trade and Industry
Transportation
Mail and Telecommunications
Labor
Construction

National Diet (elected parliament)

House of Representatives
511 seats
Members elected every 4 years
Has powers over House of
    Councillors
Can vote for no confidence
    in the Cabinet

House of Councillors
252 seats
Members elected every 6 years
(half the members every 3 years)

Make yourself at home
Important foreign visitors to
Japan stay in the government's
"Guest House." Its rooms are
decorated and furnished not
in the traditional Japanese
style, but in the traditional
Western style, to make
visitors from Western countries
feel more at home.

WAYS OF WORSHIP

The Japanese people are free to follow any religion they wish, so long as they do not break the law. The main religions are Shintoism and Buddhism.

Shinto ("the way of the gods") is Japan's traditional religion. When and how it began is not clear, but it was established well before Buddhism. Followers of Shintoism worship the natural world – animals, plants, stones, and places of great beauty. The ancestors and heroes of old are also sacred. In former times the emperor was one of its gods. To people of other religions, especially from the West, Shinto is difficult to understand. It has few set times to worship and few regular prayers to say. But it affects many aspects of Japanese daily life and thought, such as setting aside periods for meditation.

Buddhism came to Japan from its birthplace of India, through China, in about 550. It has had an enormous influence on Japanese writing, painting, architecture, and sculpture. There are many Buddhist groups or sects, including Shinsu and Zen.

Time to meditate
There are many forms of Buddhism. Some involve beliefs that heaven and earth, humans and nature are all one, and personal meditation will eventually lead to "inner peace." Time is put aside simply to sit and think.

Shinto's chief shrine
Japan has about 80,000 Shinto shrines. The chief one is the Grand Shrine at Ise, where many people lived in ancient times.

The Great Buddha

Statues of the Buddha are made all over Japan. One of the largest is the Great Buddha in the Todaiji Temple, in Nara. It is 52 feet high – the biggest bronze statue in the world. The temple is the largest wooden building in the world and one of the oldest, dating from about 750.

KEY FACTS

In a recent survey about religion:
► 112 million Japanese said their religion was Shinto.
► 89 million said they followed Buddhism.
► Almost one and a half million said they were Christians.

Since there are only 120 million Japanese, many people must have more than one religion.

Christianity crushed

Christianity was taken to Japan in 1549 by the Spaniard, Saint Francis Xavier. It was banned when Japan cut itself off from the world in the 1630s, because it was connected with foreigners and the threat of takeover. Christians were burned, tortured, and killed. This painting is *Martyrdom of the Jesuits at Nagasaki* (1662).

THE ART OF JAPAN

People all over the world admire the beauty and simplicity of Japanese art. The main features are easily recognized – strong lines, bold design, elegance, balance, and harmony with nature.

Japanese art has been through many phases, or periods. In the 6th century, Buddhism arrived in Japan and brought with it Indian and Chinese influences. During the Kamakura period of the 13th century, the Chinese religion of Zen Buddhism influenced Japanese sculpture and paintings.

The Muromachi period, from 1336 to 1603, has been called the "golden age" of Japanese art. Paintings of landscapes, trees, flowers, birds, and animals became popular subjects, and the Zen Buddhist teachings affected the way these natural subjects were portrayed. In the late Edo period, from about 1695 to 1867, colored prints made from carved wooden blocks became popular. Many prints could be made from one block, which meant that more people could afford them.

A Japanese master
Katsushika Hokusai (1760–1849) was a master painter of the countryside, with its hills, trees, animals, buildings and people. He is said to have once painted lines on a courtyard with a broom. Only when admirers climbed to the top of a nearby temple did they see that the painting was of a face – the Buddhist saint Daruma. Going from the big to the small, Hokusai also painted two sparrows on one grain of rice.

Painting waves
Ando Hiroshige is one of the most famous of all Japanese painters. By the time of his death in 1858, at the age of 61, he had produced more than 8,000 works of art. This painting, in the classical Japanese style, is called *Wind-blown waves at Shighi-ri*.

Two traditional theaters

Japanese theater is appreciated the world over. The most popular form is *Kabuki*, in which all the women characters are played by men. Many of the plays were written over 300 years ago, when Kabuki began. They tell of the adventures of warriors and noble families, or the hard life of everyday folk. The costumes and settings are splendid.

Kabuki play

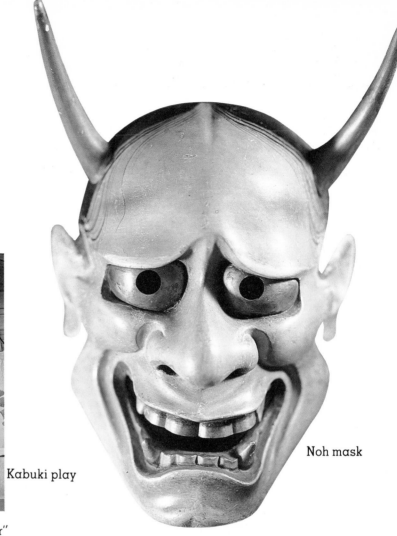

Noh mask

The special "masked theater" called *Noh* dates back over 500 years. It is a combination of acting, miming, and dancing. The players move slowly and elegantly from one position to another, wearing masks that show who they represent. There is no scenery or speech: the players use body positions and mime to tell the story.

The floating world

Woodblock designs were called *ukiyo-e*, meaning "pictures from a floating world." This print shows Japan's first railway, from Tokyo to Yokohama (1872).

IN CLASSICAL STYLE

In many areas of life, the Japanese are able to combine the traditional with the modern. This is especially true of the arts and architecture. In many cities, ancient Shinto shrines or Buddhist temples sit next to towering office buildings of glass and concrete. Traditional music is played on the *koto* (a harp-like instrument with 13 strings), the *shakuhachi* (bamboo flute) and *samsien* (like a banjo with three strings). Orchestras perform every week at concert halls, while fans of Western rock bands fill the sports arenas. Almost half the record albums sold in Japan are by foreign musicians.

Festivals are particularly important to the Japanese, and they help to keep alive the traditional beliefs and activities. Many celebrations are connected with Shintoism and Buddhism. At New Year, Shinto shrines all over Japan are filled with worshipers.

The tea ceremony
Like many other peoples, the Japanese take tea at any time of day as a refreshing drink. But the tea ceremony, *chanoyu*, is different. It is an elaborate ritual with religious meanings, which can take up to four hours. There are strict rules about what you may wear, say, and do. Guests sit quietly and admire their elegant surroundings, the beautiful tea utensils, and the grace of their hosts, while sipping *matcha* tea made from powdered green leaves. The ceremony has remained almost unchanged since the teacher Sen Rikyu devised it in the 1570s.

Gardens of great beauty

Garden and landscape design
has reached a high art in
Japan. The placings of water,
trees, flowers, and lawns, and
even small rocks and stones,
are carefully planned. The
view is balanced and pleasing
wherever you stand.

The pagoda tower

Most people recognize the
pagoda, the classical
tower-like building found in
many temples. Originally, the
design came from the Buddhist
temples in India, which was
taken up by the Chinese and
then by Japan. The 7th-century
Horyuji Temple, near Nara, is a
fine example of a pagoda.

GOING TO SCHOOL

Japan has one of the highest literacy rates in the world. This means almost everyone has learned to read, write, and handle numbers. All children must go to school from the ages of six to 15. Education is free, though after the age of 15, pupils have to buy their own school books.

The typical Japanese school is probably quite like your own school. The children have lessons in Japanese language, math, science, arts and crafts, sports and games, and music. There are also lessons in home economics, social studies (mainly history and geography), and moral studies. In secondary school there are many other subjects to learn, such as foreign languages (usually English), fine arts, classical Japanese, and handwriting skills.

The school year starts on April 1. School vacations are much the same as yours. However, the Japanese school system is very competitive. Children are encouraged to study hard and get into the university. Many spend their vacations "cramming," taking extra lessons to make sure they pass their exams.

Kindergartens and nursery schools
These are not compulsory, but many children attend from age three. Four children out of five are at kindergartens or day care centers by age five.

Elementary school
Everyone must attend from ages six to 12.

Lower secondary school
Everyone must attend from ages 12 to 15.

Upper secondary school
Pupils can leave at age 15 but nine students out of 10 stay at school until they are 18, preparing for university or college.

Universities and colleges
After upper secondary school one student in three studies for a diploma or degree. Most courses last from two to four years.

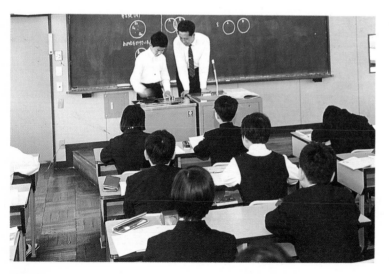

In the classroom
The teacher at his blackboard ... some children listening while others let their minds wander ... a familiar school scene almost anywhere. The Japanese writing is the only clue to which country this is.

All work and no play?
Like children everywhere, the young Japanese love to play. The main sports at school are baseball, soccer, track, and gymnastics. Bicycles and jump ropes are as popular in Japan as they are in the United States and Britain.

Smart and neat
Many young Japanese children have to wear school uniforms. The typical Japanese school is probably more formal and strict than many schools in the United States and Europe.

IN FITNESS AND IN HEALTH

Japan is a wealthy nation. Compared to countries in Africa, South America, and even nearby Southeast Asia, the Japanese earn high wages. Most of them can afford to eat properly. Nearly everyone lives in a house. Almost eight out of 10 households have a car. About 99 households in 100 have a color television.

Money also buys good health. Waste water and sewage are dealt with safely, although it might seem otherwise from the smells in hot, humid, midsummer Tokyo! Tap water is safe to drink anywhere in Japan. Generally, doctors, hospitals, and health services are among the best in the world.

But there is a price to pay. Houses, especially in towns and cities, are very small and cramped. Most health care is paid for under insurance plans. These are very complicated and some workers and companies can't really afford the payments. Pensions are run by big companies, along the same lines. All these various costs are rising, and many ordinary Japanese feel that soon they won't have enough wealth to buy good health.

Space to breathe
The average office worker's apartment near Tokyo would fit into two or three rooms of an ordinary American or European house. Because space is so limited, the living room during the day becomes a bedroom at night.

Kendo

Judo

The art of defense
Many Japanese people play a sport to stay healthy. Several forms of personal combat, or "martial arts," were developed in Japan. Some have spread around the world to become international sports. In *kendo*, the aim is to strike the opponent with a bamboo rod. This sport was developed from sword fighting. In *judo* each participant tries to throw the other to the floor using a combination of skill, balance, and strength.

40

KEY FACTS

One way to judge the health of a nation is by the life expectancy (the average age to which people live).

▶ In Japan, life expectancy is about 80 years for women and 75 years for men – among the highest in the world.

▶ In comparison, in the United States the life expectancies are about 78 years for women and 71 years for men.

▶ Such success has its problems. In Japan today, one person in 10 is over 65 years old; it will be one person in five by the year 2000. The country faces an enormous task in looking after its elderly people.

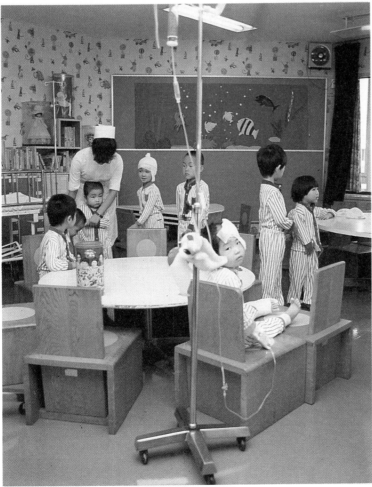

Going to the doctor

Going to the doctor or dentist in Japan is much the same as in America or Britain. The Japanese are justly proud of their medical services. There is one doctor for every 650 or so people. In some countries of Southeast Asia there is a doctor for every 50,000 people.

41

WHAT CAN WE DO TODAY?

The daily life of a Japanese family depends partly on where they live. As in America or Europe, city-dwellers often have different interests compared to those who live in the country. But shopping and housework, watching television and reading books, and playing in the park or garden are family activities everywhere.

The Japanese have several festivals during the year. The most important is on New Year. Houses are decorated with small pine trees, bamboo stems, fern leaves, oranges, and lobsters. (The lobster's bent back signifies living to an old age.) Families put on their best clothes and visit local shrines to give thanks to the gods. Afterwards they call on relatives and friends for refreshments and party games.

On other days there are many sports to play: baseball at a local field, swimming in summer, and skiing during the winter. For the luckier families who can get out to the country easily, there are walks in the fields and woods.

The fire festival

The *Wakakusayama* fire festival is held near Nara each year in mid-January. Many people come to watch an entire hillside burn. The festival began when two religious groups finally stopped fighting each other. The fire is a symbol which represents their new friendship, since it destroys the past and allows a fresh start.

Old and new

Some families decorate one or two of their rooms in the traditional style, with paper sliding doors and *tatami* grass mats on the floor. The other rooms are more modern. Almost every house has a stereo system and television.

The outdoor life

Many Japanese people have taken up outdoor activities, such as camping and boating, which have spread from other parts of the world.

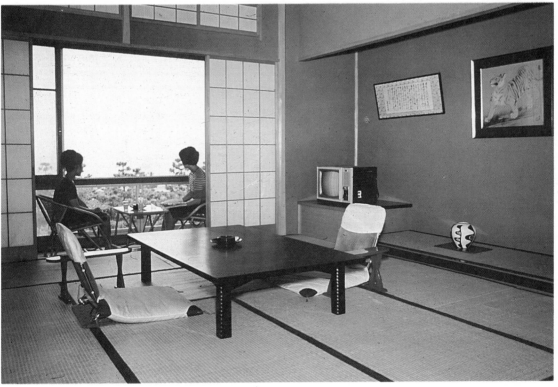

TOMORROW'S JAPAN

Japan is very successful as a manufacturing and trading nation. But at home, there are problems. Many people, especially in the cities, feel that their living conditions are too cramped and their journeys to work are too crowded. In business and in the city factories many people work long hours and see little of their families. However, the workers are encouraged to work even harder so their companies can be even more successful.

There have been improvements in recent years. City centers are less polluted with smog. Parks and nature reserves have been created where people can rest and relax. There are excellent sports and leisure centers in many towns.

The younger Japanese in particular are pressing for change. They would not mind if their country was slightly less successful as a world economic power, provided that they themselves could have a more enjoyable life.

A woman's place

Traditionally, women in Japan have stayed at home to run the house and bring up the family. Recent laws are supposed to have made women and men more equal. For example, a man and a women should earn the same wages for doing the same job. However, changing society itself seems to be a longer process. In business management, fewer than one person in 10 is a woman. And the average wage for women is less than two-thirds the wage for men.

Rising sun, setting sun

The sun sets over Tokyo Bay as the city lights begin to blaze. The Japanese people are thinking more and more of the quality of their own lives as well as the success of their nation.

The old ... and the new

The Japanese art of flower arranging (*ikebana*) has been practiced for centuries. But some Japanese people are worried about the way Western culture, with its fast food and rock albums, has influenced the young. In the future, will people still follow Japanese customs and traditions – or will the old ways fade and die?

Index

Acknowledgments
All illustrations by Ann Savage except for page 8 by Kyoko Read.
Photographic credits (a = above, b = below, m = middle, l = left,
r = right); JIC = Japan Information Center, JNTO = Japanese
National Tourist Office):
Cover al Orion Press/Zefa, bl Hunter/Zefa, ar R Halin/Zefa, br
O Warashine/Zefa; page 9 a JIC, b Hunter/Zefa; page 11 a JNTO,
b JIC; page 12 JIC; page 13 JIC; page 14 a Orion Press/Zefa, b
O Warashine/Zefa; page 15 JIC; page 17 a D Schmidt/Zefa, b
Orion Press/Zefa; page 18 JIC; page 19 JIC; page 21 JIC; page 22
Derek Cattani/Zefa; page 23 JNTO; page 25 a Steve
Kaufman/Bruce Coleman Library, b Orion Press/Zefa; page 28
Imperial War Museum; page 29 Imperial War Museum; page 30
a JIC, b JIC; page 31 Spectrum Colour Library; page 32 JIC; page
33 BPCC/Aldus Archive; page 34 V and A Museum/E T Archive;
page 35 al JIC, ar JIC, b JIC; page 36 Orion Press/Zefa; page 37
M Thonig/Zefa; page 38 JIC; page 39 a D Cattani/Zefa, b T La
Tona/Zefa; page 41 a JIC, b Bill Tingey; page 42 JNTO; page 43 a
JNTO, b JNTO; page 44 JIC; page 45 a Richard/Zefa, b JNTO.